Saving Our Water

by Margaret L. Cuffney

Scott Foresman
is an imprint of

Glenview, Illinois • Boston, Massachusetts • Mesa, Arizona
Shoreview, Minnesota • Upper Saddle River, New Jersey

We live in a watery world. In fact, about 70 percent of Earth's surface is covered with water. There is even more water *beneath* the surface of our planet.

Plants, animals, and people need water in order to survive. Unfortunately, some of Earth's water supplies are **polluted**. Polluted water is not safe for people or animals to drink. It is not safe to use for growing crops. Polluted water is also not safe for the animals that make their homes in it.

Water Pollution

How does water become polluted? Water can become polluted in many ways. Some pollution happens naturally. For example, heavy rain can carry soil into a river or lake. This usually isn't a serious problem because the soil will settle at the bottom of the river or lakebed.

Other pollution is caused by people. Many farmers use chemicals to kill weeds and insects that harm crops. Homeowners also use chemicals to keep their lawns green. And cities spread salt on roads to melt ice in the winter. The rain washes some of these substances off the plants and roads and into the soil and nearby rivers and lakes. This can make the water unsafe to drink.

Chemicals that help this corn grow can end up in our water supply.

Another possible source of water pollution is wastewater from homes and businesses. Water from bathtubs, toilets, washing machines, and kitchen sinks is filled with bacteria and other impurities. Factories also produce large amounts of wastewater. Sometimes this water contains harmful chemicals.

If this polluted water soaks into the soil or flows into a river or stream, it will harm the water supply. When water soaks into the soil, it becomes part of an underground water supply called groundwater. Most of our drinking water comes from groundwater, so it is important to keep this valuable resource clean.

Wastewater can pollute our drinking supply.

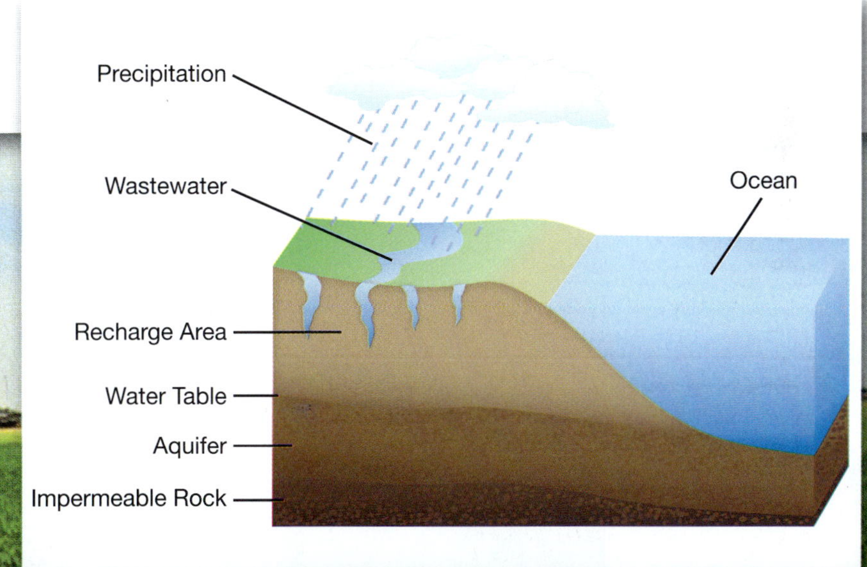

Some of the water that falls to the earth will become "surface runoff," or water that flows overland. Surface runoff in one area will usually drain to the same place. The region of land and water that drains into one place is called a **watershed**. Any region, no matter how small, can be considered a watershed if it drains to one place. Even a footprint in the sand can be considered a watershed. Smaller watersheds make up larger watersheds.

All rivers eventually empty into an ocean. About a third of the water that falls to the earth as precipitation will become surface runoff and return to the ocean.

On its way to the ocean, river water flows through farmland, towns, and cities. In some places, the water may pick up pollutants. These pollutants will end up in the ocean.

This watershed is comprised of the area of land that drains into this river.

Air Pollution

Exhaust from cars, buses, and other vehicles contains chemicals that pollute the air. Smoke from factories and power plants pollutes the air too. Even heating your home can cause air pollution.

Most cars, factories, power plants, and homes depend on **fossil fuels** for power and heat. Some fossil fuels are gasoline, oil, and coal. Burning fossil fuels releases harmful chemicals into the air.

How does polluted air affect our water supply? To answer this question, let's look at how the water cycle works.

Unused gas and steam escape into the air from car engines.

Water from oceans, lakes, and rivers **evaporates** and turns into **water vapor.** Water from the leaves of trees and other plants becomes water vapor too. Harmful chemicals in the air will dissolve in the water vapor, causing it to become polluted.

As the temperature of the air cools, the water vapor condenses and forms tiny droplets of water. When enough droplets collect, they form clouds. Eventually, the polluted water droplets fall to the Earth as polluted **precipitation** in the form of rain, snow, sleet, or hail. So polluted air means polluted precipitation.

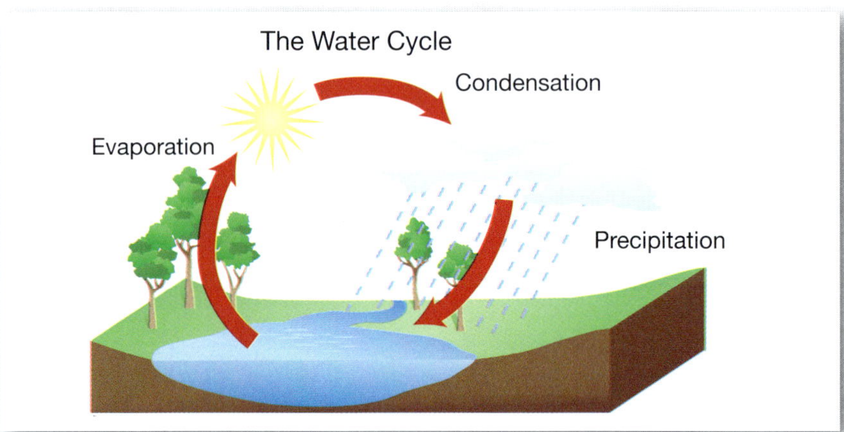

If there is pollution in the air, it can show up later as pollution in the rain, which will, in turn, pollute lakes and rivers.

Acid occurs naturally in soil and rocks. It is found in lake water and rainwater. In normal amounts, acid is not a problem.

However, **acid rain** is a serious problem. Acid rain is rain that contains far more than the usual amount of acid.

How does acid get into the rain? Chemicals from car exhaust and factory smoke enter the atmosphere. Then they combine with water vapor in the air. This produces acid. The acid falls back to the earth as acid rain. It pollutes the soil by adding too much acid. Acid rain also pollutes rivers, streams, lakes, and other bodies of water.

This smoke may contain harmful chemicals.

Effects of Pollution

What happens when the water supply becomes polluted? One major problem is that polluted water cannot be used for drinking or watering crops.

Another problem is that polluted water affects animal habitats. Chemicals that are harmful to people are also dangerous for animals. Fish that swim in polluted water end up taking some of these chemicals into their bodies. This can cause large numbers of fish to die. It can also make the fish unsafe for people to eat. For example, a harmful chemical called mercury can be found in ocean water. Some tuna have high levels of mercury in their bodies, which can make people sick when they eat the tuna.

Plants and animals pay the price for water pollution. A healthy body of water has a natural balance that makes life possible. This water receives enough sunlight to allow plants to grow. These plants produce oxygen, which marine animals breathe.

When water is badly polluted, this natural balance is upset. Chemicals in the water may kill certain plants. The animals that depend on those plants may die as well.

Which of these habitats looks like a healthy place for animals to live?

Acid rain can kill trees such as pine and maple trees. It is also dangerous for fish. In some areas, lakes once filled with fish are almost empty. Scientists believe that this is because of high acid levels in the lakes.

Scientists collect rain to measure the amount of acid in it. Then they check the weather patterns to see how far the acid has traveled. Scientists have found that chemicals from power plants in one area can fall as acid rain hundreds of miles away!

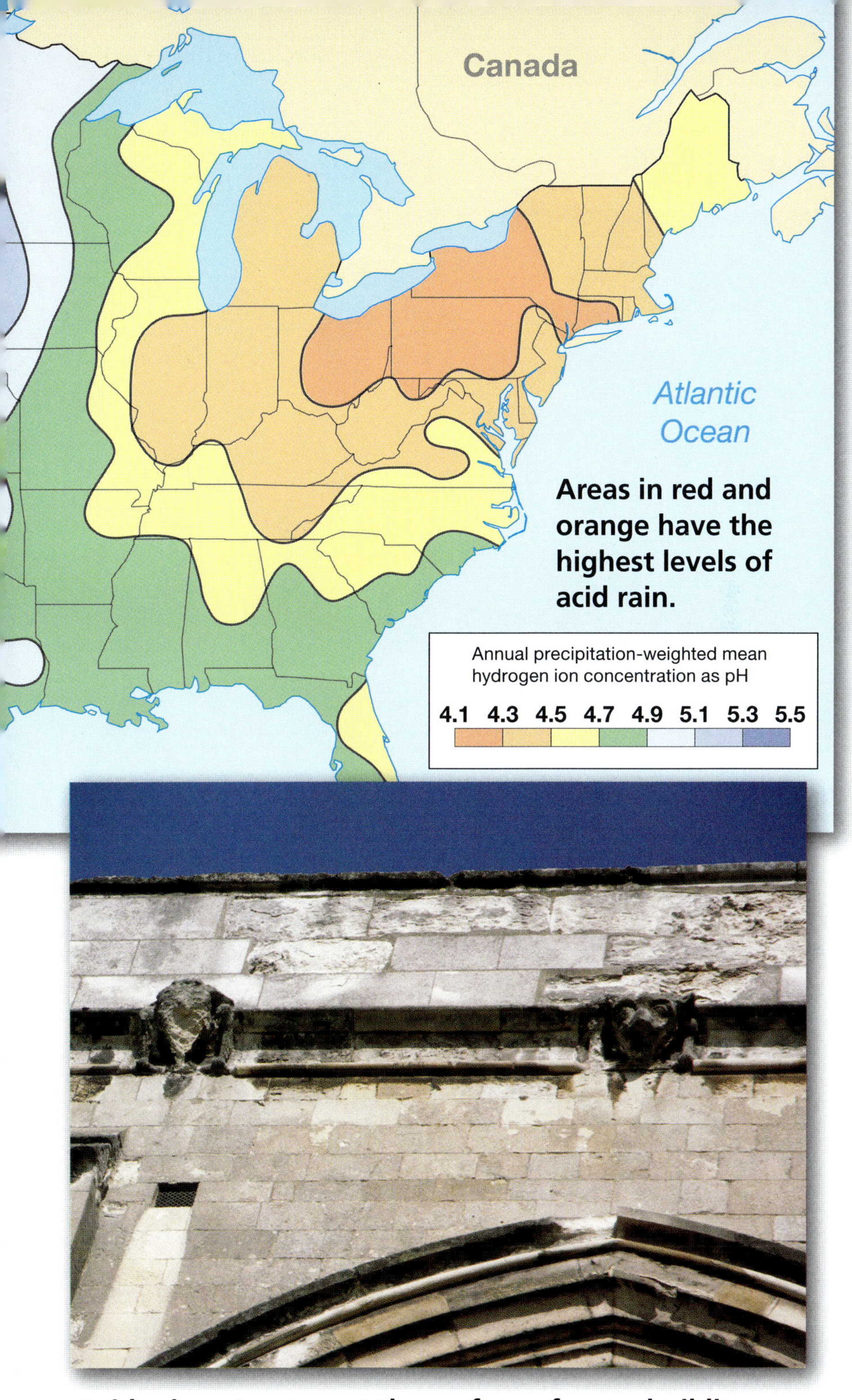

Acid rain eats away at the surface of some buildings.

Reducing Pollution

Cleaner air means cleaner water. So what can we do to keep our air clean? People around the world are working to find an answer to this question right now.

One answer is to reduce the amount of pollution caused by burning fossil fuels. In the United States and other places, there are laws that factories and power plants must obey. The laws require these businesses to use special equipment to monitor the amount of chemicals that escape into the air.

Public transportation, such as subways and commuter trains, helps keep the air clean too. The fewer people that drive, the less gasoline is burned. Using less gasoline means less pollution in the air.

In many places drivers must have their cars inspected regularly. One thing inspectors check for is the amount of pollution that the car is releasing into the air. Each car must adhere to regulations that limit the amount of pollution released.

What if everyone on this subway drove a car to work instead? Would that mean more pollution or less pollution?

Another way to use less fossil fuel is to replace it with other energy sources. **Hybrid** cars run partially on electricity. This means these cars do not need as much gasoline. As a result, their exhaust causes less pollution. Inventors also are working on ideas such as electric cars that do not use gasoline at all.

Scientists are looking for better ways to provide heat and power to homes and businesses too. Solar panels are one possibility. They produce energy from sunlight and do not release harmful chemicals into the air. The wind also can be used to produce clean power.

Solar panels capture the sun's heat and use it to heat this house.

Wind farms use the power of wind to create electricity.

Keeping the air clean is one way to save our water supply. We also need to be sure water does not get polluted in other ways.

Many industries use a lot of water during manufacturing. They need to get rid of the wastewater that is created. Industries often do this by piping the wastewater into nearby rivers, streams, or oceans. The United States and other nations now have laws that require factories to treat, or clean, wastewater before getting rid of it.

Impurities in this water will end up in our water supply.

Preserving the wetlands also is important. A wetland is an area of land where water covers the soil or is near the surface of the soil, such as a marsh or swamp.

Wetlands are very important to our water supply. Wetlands act like sponges and soak up water. This helps prevent floods. It also keeps soil from running off and entering rivers and streams.

Wetlands act as natural filters. As water slowly flows through a wetland, substances that can cause pollution are removed from the water.

One danger to wetlands is housing or business development. Some wetlands have been filled in so that homes could be built. Today there are laws that protect wetlands. In many places people cannot build near a wetland.

Many animals live in wetland habitats.

How can you help protect and save our water supply? Conserving water is one important step you can take. But you also can help prevent the pollution of our water supply. Never pour substances like paint or chemical cleaners down the drain. Don't dump them outside on the ground either. Many communities have special waste disposal days on which they collect these substances. Then workers dispose of them safely.

There are safe ways to dispose of harmful chemicals.

You can help keep litter from polluting our water supply!

It also is important not to litter. Remember that anything you throw on the ground could end up getting washed into a nearby body of water.

Another way to save our water supply is by using your muscles. Walk or bike to the park instead of asking for a ride. You will be keeping the harmful chemicals in car exhaust from entering the air.

We can't live without clean water. So we all need to do our part!

Let's recycle!

We can all do our part to protect the planet from pollution. One way that you can keep pollutants from entering our water supply is by recycling. Here is an activity you can do today to get started!

1. Gather information about what kinds of things can be recycled where you live. You should be able to find a list of recyclables on your town's website.
2. Record the information that you've gathered.
3. Share what you've learned with your classmates. Make a recycling poster to hang in the school cafeteria or in your classroom.
4. Include information such as what can be recycled and what cannot be recycled. Your poster should show other students how and where to recycle.

Glossary

acid rain *n.* rain containing acids, formed by pollutants from the burning of fossil fuels

exhaust *n.* the burned gasses that escape from an engine

evaporates *v.* changes from a liquid into a gas

fossil fuels *n.* any fuels found in the earth and formed from the remains of things that lived millions of years ago, such as coal, oil, and natural gas

hybrid *adj.* of mixed origin

polluted *adj.* dirtied or made impure

precipitation *n.* act or process of falling from the air in the form of rain, snow, etc.

watershed *n.* the region drained by one river system

water vapor *n.* water in a gaseous state and below boiling temperature, as distinct from steam